# New Kids on the Block

Anne M. Raso

**Modern Publishing**

A Division of Unisystems, Inc.
New York, New York 10022

Printed in the U.S.A.

D0044063

Front Cover Photos of Joe, Jon and Danny by Robin Platzer
Front Cover Photos of Donnie and Jordan by Ernie Paniccioli
Back Cover Photo by Ernie Paniccioli
Book Design by Kate Gartner

Book Number: 10515
ISBN Number: 0-87449-823-6

Printed in the U.S.A.

# Contents

Introduction .......................................5

The Right Stuff.....................................7

Donnie Wahlberg..............................15

Danny Wood .....................................21

Jon Knight...........................................25

Joe McIntyre.......................................31

Jordan Knight.....................................37

From around the Block to around the
World—Life on the Road ...................43

Friends First . . . and Forever .............49

"Tough" Times Ahead ......................53

Vital Stats You Can't Live Without .......56

New Kids Quiz ...................................59

"Blockbusters": A New Kids' Discography
and Videography ............................62

Although the New Kids on the Block are from Boston, they are well-known all over the world. From left to right are Danny Wood, Donnie Wahlberg, Joe McIntyre, Jordan Knight and Jon Knight. *Ernie Paniccioli*

# Introduction

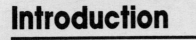

The New Kids on the Block are moving in on the pop scene in a big, big way. Not only is their second LP, *Hangin' Tough,* double platinum, but they've had five big hits in the past year.

And just *who* are the New Kids on the Block? Simply put, the New Kids are five talented Boston boys named Joe McIntyre, Jordan Knight, Jon Knight, Donnie Wahlberg and Danny Wood. What sets them apart from other singing groups is that they're young (ages 16 to 20) and have a sincere, streetwise attitude that appeals to teens of both sexes. The fact that Joe, Jordan, Jon, Donnie and Danny are "real" kids makes fans feel like they know them.

In this book, you'll find out the real story of the New Kids' rise to fame, what unique personality traits each "Kid" possesses and what's in their very rosy future. By the time you're done reading, you'll feel like you're a member of the group, or at least a very good friend.

Read on and enjoy! It's the "right stuff" on the "right group" for the 1990s!

Out of more than 500 young men who auditioned for the forthcoming group, Danny, Donnie, Joe, Jordan and Jon were viewed as the most talented by the group's managers.
*Ernie Paniccioli*

# The Right Stuff
## *The Real New Kids Story*

**T**he New Kids were "put together" by two very talented Boston area music biz people: personal manager Mary Alford and famed record producer/songwriter Maurice Starr (who was responsible for New Edition's initial success).

How Mary and Maurice got the idea to put together a teen singing group is an amusing story, for their paths crossed totally by accident one day while they were both driving to a Roslindale, Massachusetts, shopping center. Mary had known Maurice from hanging out in the fertile Boston music scene for 10 years, and that day they met up in 1984 proved to be a monumental one in pop history. In conversation, Mary said she had been thinking about putting together a pop version of New Edition for a couple of months. Interestingly enough, Maurice admitted that he had been thinking about doing the same thing ever since New Edition took off in a big way the year before.

Mary went home to Dorchester, happy knowing that she had "touched base" with Maurice, someone she had long admired and who is considered a legend in black music circles. But she never would've guessed that Maurice would be calling in a few days asking her to be the "Gal Friday" (personal assistant) on his little top secret project.

Mary and Maurice set out to make a white counterpart for New Edition and quickly set out auditioning boys by placing ads in music business trade papers, hanging up signs and even asking boys in their neighborhoods if they could sing!

Mary did all the "hands-on" work, calling up each boy who sent in a resume and picture. The finalists had to be strong on three counts: age (they had to be under 18), singing skills and dancing ability. (Good looks didn't hurt either!)

It took Mary six months to audition the 500-plus boys who applied, and the first guy she picked to join was Donnie Wahlberg, who was then 15. What set Donnie apart from the other 500 guys who auditioned? Well, Mary couldn't resist his sweet and considerate personality or his incredible audition, where he did a 10-minute impersonation of the "Gloved One," Michael Jackson.

The group came together almost magically at that point, for Donnie started to seek out group members himself and had no problem recruiting school friends Danny Wood (also 15) and Jordan Knight (14). Jordan was quick to point out that he had a cute and talented older brother named Jon (then 16) who would be anxious to audition. Jon passed his audition with flying colors!

So the core of the New Kids was put together by spring '85, except for one problem: they needed a fifth guy who could be a lead singer. According to group insiders, they were looking for a "Donnie Osmond" type who could sing. They chose 13-year-old Joe McIntyre.

Next up on the agenda was choosing the name for the group. Mary and Maurice must've tossed around 50 names by the time they came up with Nynuk, the Kids' original moniker.

The bizarre name stuck for a couple of months in mid-1985, as the kids entered a Boston recording studio and "canned" four songs for a demo tape. One of the numbers was a Maurice Starr composition called "New Kids on the Block." When the boys realized that the lyrics were almost autobiographical, they wanted to change their name. Maurice was reluctant to give up the strange name he had given them, but even a genius like Maurice had to admit "New Kids" was a more appropriate choice.

And so the New Kids were officially "born"— now, all they needed was a major record deal. In the second half of '85, Mary and Maurice shipped the four-song demo tape to all the major record labels, to a generally positive response. Columbia Records—the biggest record label in the country—was anxious to sign the Kids, and how could the group resist joining up! The boys completed the papers in January 1986 and jumped for joy that they were affiliated with CBS. They couldn't wait to enter the studio to record their first single as a "major recording group." The name of the song was "Be My Girl," and it was done in the traditional teen bubble-gum style. While it never became a national hit, it did become a local hit thanks to the support it received from dance club deejays.

From the time the single was released in April

9

Before the group was named the New Kids, they were called Nynuk. From left to right are Joe, Jon, Donnie, Danny and Jordan. *Ernie Paniccioli*

1986, the guys went on a full-speed-ahead mission to make themselves one of the most talked-about groups in the land. In early to mid-summer, they recorded their self-titled debut album, which came out at the end of the year, and although they didn't have one album on the shelves during the summer of '86, they still managed to get themselves quality "gigs." For instance, on July 4, 1986, they performed as part of the Statue of Liberty festivities in Manhattan's Battery Park. They sang "New Kids on the Block" for the first time in the Big Apple, and the kids attending the show really felt the group's stage presence and knew that they were going to be big someday.

Next up was another really hot gig that even the most seasoned pop veteran would've envied—opening for the legendary Four Tops at the annual

Kite Festival in Dorchester, Massachusetts. Believe it or not, that show was followed up with an opening slot for Lisa Lisa & Cult Jam at the "over 21" club called 9 Lansdowne in Boston.

Columbia released two more singles from the Kids' LP: the cutesy "Stop It Girl" and a clever remake of the 1970 Delfonics' soul hit, "Didn't I Blow Your Mind?" While these records were certainly well produced and executed—not to mention a novelty for the period in pop history in which they were released—they didn't even make a dent on the pop charts. However, the R&B audience—the New Kids' original fans—helped the songs make it into the Hot 100 on the black charts.

While the Kids spent late '86 and early '87 promoting their debut LP, they couldn't wait to get into the recording studio and do their second album—which was to be called *Hangin' Tough.* They spent a full year poring over material with Maurice. According to Jon Knight, "We were looking for material that was more 'street' and less bubble gum. The last album was what we called 'kid funk' and this album is just 'street'—or what Jordan simply calls 'hip.'"

Jordan adds, "The last album went one way, to one crowd. This album goes to everybody, it's not just R&B." Ironically, like its predecessor, *Hangin' Tough* initially dazzled just the black audience. But then the group found itself on tour with Tiffany in the summer of '88 to support the album and its first single, "Please Don't Go Girl." The tour with the redheaded pop singer certainly helped the group's career, because by the time fall came around, "Girl" was in the Top 10.

While they were busy on the Tiffany tour, they hardly had time to realize that their second single

11

off the *Hangin' Tough* LP, "You Got It (The Right Stuff)," took a 20-point leap on the charts between the first and second weeks of November. That's a rare feat, which the Kids learned when well-known music biz veterans pointed it out to them. Shortly thereafter, the video for "The Right Stuff" was released and received heavy airplay on MTV—and no wonder, since the high budget production was directed by Doug Nichols who directed the Cars and Patti LaBelle's videos.

The boys also headlined at some small venues at this point in their career. During a date in Detroit, they took time out to tape a Nickelodeon show called *Block Party,* where they actually hosted a party at a bowling alley for the lucky winner of a New Kids contest.

In late November '88, the Kids went on a week-long promotional tour of Japan, where they taped a series of commercials for Sony.

They were back in their native B-town on November 21 with extreme cases of jet lag, but they managed to do a benefit performance for their hometown Police Athletic League and shortly thereafter appeared with the Pointer Sisters and Jeffrey Osbourne at the 60th anniversary of the Boston Garden.

If that wasn't enough, the Kids made a return trip to Hawaii over Christmas to be greeted again by thousands of screaming fans at the airport. They played at several of the Hawaiian Islands and then came back to the continental States to perform on the nationally televised United Cerebral Palsy telethon. It was their third consecutive year on the telethon and they performed their two hits.

In February, the Kids were slated for another four-month tour with Tiffany, and yet another hit off their album, "I'll Be Loving You (Forever)," was released and quickly went into the Top Five. It was no wonder that Columbia couldn't wait to release the title track of their LP—which was about to go platinum—as the next single a couple of months later.

September 1989 was a banner month in the group's history, for two major phenomena occurred: the boys found themselves in the position to headline at arenas, and the album *Hangin' Tough* and its title track topped the album and singles charts, respectively.

And let's not forget that a new single, "Cover Girl," hit the charts in early September, just as "Hangin' Tough" was beginning to fade. To further add to the New Kids hysteria currently breaking out all over the world, the Kids released a Christmas album—aptly titled *Merry, Merry Christmas*—on September 19. It was released a bit prematurely considering the holiday season was three months away, but when a group is as hot as the New Kids, record retailers are justifiably anxious to cash in. They've got the right stuff—and they know how to use it!

Donnie is considered the "take charge" member of the group.
*Ernie Paniccioli*

# Donnie Wahlberg

*The Street Kid with the Heart of Gold!*

**W**hat's Donnie Wahlberg really like? That's a question that would take days to answer, because he's a pretty complex guy—or what *he* likes to call "intense." Donnie's strongest quality is his amazing ability to make friends with many people.

Donnie is from a superlarge family: he's got five brothers and three sisters. He says that growing up in a big family has made him more considerate of other people's feelings and that he's never been lonely for a minute.

Donnie's family has been very supportive of his career, and sometimes his sisters help answer fan mail. Donnie explains, "I wouldn't be anywhere without my parents or brothers and sisters—they have just been great through all this. I admit that I miss my mom when I'm out on the road, and when she shows up for a show, I can't help but run up to her and give her a great big kiss. I know it sounds

Donnie comes from a very supportive family. He says he misses his mom when he's on the road. *Ernie Paniccioli*

corny, but she's the greatest! I wouldn't be here without her!"

Donnie is the real "take-charge" member of the New Kids. If there's a problem, he's the one to try and mend it. Donnie's enthusiasm for his work helps the boys keep going when they're tired.

The Dorchester native (who's named after his father) has a tendency to be very analytical and wants to know how everything works—that's why when he's in the recording studio, he can't help but question producer Maurice Starr and the engineers about their jobs. Even though his star has just risen as a performer, this guy just can't wait to help others—he's producing a group of neighborhood rappers called the Northside Posse, and hopefully, they'll have a record on the shelves next year.

A Leo born on August 17, 1969, Donnie has his serious moments, although from seeing the funny faces he makes in photos, you'd think he was a total clown. To say he takes his career seriously is an understatement—he hopes to show off his drumming abilities on a future New Kids' record, and he coproduced and cowrote the tune "My Favorite Girl" with Maurice, Jordan and Danny.

When asked what famous person he's most like, Donnie will answer the Cookie Monster. He may not be blue and fuzzy, but Donnie loves cookies (especially Oreos) and has lots of neighborhood friends. He's also got a lot of the Cookie Monster's famous lines down pat and uses them onstage and on the New Kids telephone hotline.

Donnie has helped the group through many onstage disasters, including technical difficulties. He explains that during one personal appearance in New York, they had to lip-sync to prerecorded tracks, "and suddenly the music went off. I suggested we sing a cappella. It worked out pretty well!''

Donnie's also on top of tour schedules and is a kind of assistant road manager to the Kids' *real* road manager, Peter Work. Peter's a busy guy—besides working with the Kids, he manages a hot new New York rap group called the Def Duo—so he needs a guy like Donnie to occasionally "mind the store."

In his spare time, Donnie can be found sitting in the "quiet room" of the tour bus sipping a glass of water and watching movies on the VCR. Sometimes he sits back there with some of the other boys and signs albums and pictures for giveaways at local radio stations or in national magazines. When he doesn't feel like being cooped up, he gathers the guys together for a walk to the mall or a rough game of basketball. Donnie is challenging the guys in New Edition to join the New Kids for a celebrity basketball game, with all proceeds going to the Kids' favorite charity, United Cerebral Palsy.

All in all, Donnie is a really "together" kid, and he's the kind of boy whom everyone should have as an older brother. He's caring, kind and considerate. The other guys refer to him as the "soul" of the New Kids.

Donnie likes to buy clothes and probably makes the biggest fashion statement in the group. He loves the contrast of black and gold and often combines those colors in his outfits. Donnie is like a chameleon when it comes to his clothes and hair. Sometimes he looks as if he belongs in Run-D.M.C., sometimes he looks as if he belongs in prep school, and other times he looks far-out 'n' funky in ripped-up jeans and an early '60s suit jacket.

Donnie uses his celebrity status to speak out

against drugs. He remarks, "We don't like drugs . . . we're strongly against them . . . especially crack, because it's an epidemic. Crack's really bad. Drugs are deadly—but crack is the worst. We're strongly against it." Donnie has said time and time again that if the group can someday fit it into their busy schedule, he'd like them to go to schools and speak out against drug use. "I think kids should be educated about drugs at as early an age as possible—even seven or eight isn't too young. You don't know what's going on in the inner city. The sooner they're educated, the better."

When asked what his ultimate goal is, he responds with a smile, "I just want to see us stick together through thick and thin. I love these guys—we're like brothers!"

Donnie is a "brother" to everyone who crosses his path—no wonder the other Kids refer to him as the "soul" of the group.

Danny says the best part of the entertainment business is the opportunity to meet different people. *Ernie Paniccioli*

# Danny Wood
## *Stubborn but Sweet!*

**F**irst impressions die hard, and the first impression that everyone has of Danny Wood is that he's the quietest guy in the world. Nothing could be further from the truth—when he's hangin' with the rest of the New Kids or with a bunch of good friends, Danny's a chatterbox.

Ask Danny what made him what he is today, and he'll have an answer similar to Donnie's—"My mom!" He adds with a chuckle, "My biggest message to the fans is always be nice to your mom 'cause she's always there for you and she deserves it!"

Danny (who's named after his dad, just like Donnie) says he can get along with people from all different backgrounds "as long as they're friendly and have a good sense of humor."

"I like meeting people," he says. "One of the best things about being in this business is getting to meet all different kinds of people . . . but of course our favorite kind of person is a New Kids fan!"

Danny says that he's proud of the group's streetwise image. He likes the fact that they're stars who are *real* kids. Danny explains, "We're from the streets. Kids can relate to our image. Before we got into the group I was into the streets—not the drug scene or anything. I was into the break-dancing scene. Joining the group was something like basketball—if you play basketball you can stay off the streets, you can set a goal. Music has made a goal for us."

But handsome, high-cheekboned Danny has future plans outside of performing. He'd like to get into the behind-the-scenes action of recording. He reveals, "I'd like to be an engineer in the studio, and maybe a writer . . . but right now, singing comes first. Why do I want to be an engineer?, you ask. Well, it just seems really interesting to me because when we're in the studio in front of the board, I want to know what every single knob does!"

Danny's got another talent besides singing and messing with the knobs in the control room—he's been playing keyboards for a whole year. Jordan is the group member who inspired him to take up the "88s," for the younger Knight brother really knows how to tickle the ivories.

Danny says he's been more heavily influenced by black music than by rock 'n' roll. "I've been very influenced by singles that have popped up on the black charts . . . a lot of dance songs are what I really like. I've always been in touch with black music since I've always gone to mostly black schools. That music is my whole life."

Being a Taurean born on May 14, 1970, Danny

knows his faults and often reflects on them. He reveals his biggest personality flaw: "I'm really stubborn. I'm not adventurous at all. I like to play it safe and do what I know best."

What Danny does best is work hard, according to the other guys. They all agree that Danny is indeed the hardest-working member of the group. They call him the guy with the most energy. He does everything in a quick "puff" of energy—that's why the other Kids have nicknamed him "Puff McCloud!"

What does this black-haired 19-year-old do in his spare time? Well, besides practicing on his Korg keyboard, he roots for all the Boston sports teams. On Sunday nights (if it doesn't interfere with a concert date), Danny can be found hanging out with Jordan in a hotel room watching *America's Most Wanted.* Danny likes to joke that with all the traveling the New Kids do, they should've apprehended one of the "10 Most Wanted" criminals by now!

Danny has a sincere love for his fans and still blushes when girls scream his name. He's modest about his looks and, believe it or not, doesn't think he is good-looking at all! He can be very critical of himself and often says that he thinks he is too short (he's 5'7 1/2") and has too square of a head!

Danny has a unique philosophy toward being in a hard-touring, successful singing group. He says, "I just take things one day at a time and try to learn as much as possible." His favorite expressions are "Hang tough" and "I'm outta here," and he uses them both about 10 times per day.

Danny is a real daydreamer and often tells fans he meets to "hold on to your dreams." He thinks that everyone should try to be their best so that they feel good about themselves. He says,

"You've got to love yourself before anybody else can love you." He also urges fans to stay in school "because you won't make anything out of yourself if you don't."

According to Donnie, Danny is the most outgoing member of the group. He says, "Danny has one of those personalities that everyone likes; he makes everyone feel really comfortable and he doesn't put on any airs. We put our foreheads together before each show, hoping that some of Danny's energy will rub off—not to mention his great dancing."

Overall, "Puff McCloud" is one happy guy! He's living out his dream at a very young age, and, more important, he's helping other kids by making music they enjoy and speaking out against drugs via the Governor's Alliance Against Drugs (which all the Kids participate in when they're at home for a few days or more).

"I just want this to continue," says Danny, "and for it always to be this fun. It feels good to have so many people love you! It's cool—the fans give us energy. The guys wonder where I get all my energy, and the truth is that it rubs off from all the wonderful fans out there. Keep up the dream!"

# Jon Knight
## *The Oldest Kid on the Block*

**B**orn on November 29, 1968, Jon Knight is the oldest member of the New Kids, and he possesses the very strong Sagittarian trait of loving to travel. That's a good thing, because the New Kids travel more than any other band in the world, and probably 100 times what the normal person travels in a lifetime!

Another Sagittarian trait he possesses is being very open-minded. He likes all kinds of movies, television shows and music—the only thing he stays away from is heavy metal!

Jon's major function in the group—besides producing those smooth tenor vocals—is being the "big brother." Jordan Knight talks about Jon's "brotherly" ways: "Jon is always telling us to be good and to mind our manners. Like, if we're at the dinner table, he'll tell us to take our elbows off the table and stuff like that!"

At 5'11" and 160 pounds, Jon is an inch taller and five pounds heavier than Jordan, but they're

25

In addition to being the oldest member in the group, Jon also is considered the "big brother." *Ernie Paniccioli*

close enough in size to share clothes. Both brothers love jean jackets and vests, and exchange them often—but it's Jordan who takes longer to return the borrowed items.

Jon says his biggest fault is complaining too much and that he's sometimes a "pain in the neck." One thing he *never* complains about, however, is the success the New Kids have been having lately. "No one can deny that it's a dream come true," he says, "and I hope we continue until we can no longer sing."

Jon says that he really enjoys having his brother in the group, but thinks it's strange when people say they look alike because he thinks that they don't look the least bit similar except for their noses and hair color!

The Knight boys have always been really close, and a lot of that has to do with the fact that they're from a large family—four boys and two girls! Their interest in singing came when they were still in grade school: they sang every Sunday in their church choir for many years and then progressed to singing at local birthday parties and other special occasions.

In his spare time, Jon likes to watch comedy movies, especially ones that star Eddie Murphy. He also loves to watch TV and likes a variety of shows, from *Miami Vice* to *The Cosby Show.*

Jon likes to dance as much as he loves to sing, and he often practices at home with his brother. He's anxious to learn all the hot new dance steps from the neighborhood kids every time he goes home, but he admits he loves a lot of the old steps made famous by groups like The Temptations and The Jackson Five. "We've kind of revised the old dances and made them new," he explains. "We all have good ideas for dances, and we put them together with a little help from our choreographer, Tyrone Proctor."

Jon likes girls who are independent and successful, so he definitely never gets accused of being a chauvinist! He admits that the girls he likes have pretty much the same personality traits as he has. Jon says, "I don't really believe that opposites attract; I believe the 'alikes' attract."

Jon says the only problems he has with being famous are a lack of privacy—although he definitely doesn't mind signing autographs, even at inopportune times—and being tired a lot. He loves to sleep and, unfortunately, doesn't get more than five hours a night on the road. "When I get back home," he says, "the first thing that happens is that my head hits the pillow and I don't wake up until the next afternoon!"

Jon and Jordan's parents have always supported their sons' careers and pushed them to sing at an early age. They're very proud of their sons' accomplishments and claim that they always knew that the boys were going to "make it" in show business.

Jon appreciates all the people involved in putting the New Kids "on the map," and that includes his real family and the Kids' "business family," made up of Columbia Records' executives and the management team at Dick Scott Entertainment in New York. One of his favorites from the Dick Scott team is road manager Peter Work, whom he relies on for all his on-the-road needs, from finding a soda machine in a hotel lobby to updating his tour itinerary. So it's no wonder that

Jon's favorite expression is "Where's Peter?" He doesn't make a move without him!

Jon says he's a kid with simple tastes. He likes nothing better than the strawberry shakes served at McDonald's and he's got simple tastes when it comes to going out. A quiet walk around the more scenic parts of Boston or a quiet dinner is just fine with him.

When asked to look to the future, the only thing that Jon says is, "They've started to call us 'The Five Hardest-Working Kids in Show Business,' and I always want us to be like that. As long as the work's there, I'll do it," Jon says.

Although he is the youngest member in the group, Joe carries most of the musical burden. *Robin Platzer, Images*

# Joe McIntyre
## *The Youngest Kid on the Block*

Joe McIntyre, the youngest member of the New Kids, will never forget his audition for the group for as long as he lives! After all, he knew that if he got into the Kids, he would have to "carry" most of the musical burden.

"I tried out on Father's Day—June 15, 1985. Mary (Alford) picked me up and I was really scared. I went to Maurice's house and tried out. I sang some of the songs they were about to record, and afterwards we got in the car and Mary said, 'Well, do you want to be in the group? You've got the part!' And I said, 'Yeah, here I am,' and we recorded the songs."

How did a nice kid like Joe—who is perhaps the quintessential all-American boy—wind up in show business in the first place? He says that it never really "happened"—he just fell into it due to the fact that his sisters are show-biz oriented (one even appeared on *The Guiding Light*). "I never really thought about it. I just got the part," he says.

Joe reminisces about his earliest contact with show business; "I sang in a big group—about 70 kids—when I was six; it was part of the Neighborhood Children's Theatre of Boston. I was in the group until I was 11 or 12, and then I heard about the auditions for what was to become the New Kids."

Although he's a really down-to-earth guy who's remained the same through his great success, Joe admits that his old buddies treat him a little differently. "I still have the same friends, but they're always asking me questions about the (*Hangin' Tough*) album—so I'm getting more attention. In school, I get more attention too, once people realize what I'm doing. It's changed a little bit, but I have the same friends and I have the same personality as before I joined the group."

And what's Joe's favorite part of being in the New Kids? "The (recording) studio and the shows—they're the core of what we do. It's good being in the studio, but I'd say that the shows are a little easier. They're really fun."

Joe likes to joke that his family is "not normal," because he's got seven sisters and one brother and home life can often be like a circus. His sisters are actresses who do a lot of commercial work, and, as vice president of the Boston Bricklayers Union, Joe's dad appeared in a commercial for Governor Michael Dukakis in 1986. Joe's mom holds down a job as a secretary and helps organize the New Kids Fan Club.

A Capricorn born on December 31, 1972, Joe has an extremely positive attitude toward life and always has a smile on his face. Fans wonder if it bothers him being the youngest member of the group, and he responds, "Only sometimes . . ."

He will admit, however, that he is the most teased member of the group. "Jon likes to get on my case a lot. But if the group teases me, it's not because I'm little, it's just because I'm Joe."

Joe's life is different from the rest of the New Kids because he still has a year of high school left. He has to get up early every morning while on the road to study with his tutor while the other guys are fast asleep.

He describes his typical touring day: "I'd probably get up early 'cause I usually have school around 8 A.M. I'd probably get breakfast, then we'd go to a mall or something, then go to a sound check, practice, play around on our instruments and do stuff like that. Then we'd go back to the hotel to relax . . . just chill out and get something to eat. Then, it'd probably be around six o'clock. We'd probably take showers, go back to the venue, get ready and do a show. And then whatever happens after a show is up in the air, but we never go out to clubs. A lot of the time we go back to our rooms and go back to sleep! Sometimes during the day we meet up with fans and they take us around. I love touring—and I don't mind living out of a suitcase . . . as a matter of fact, I never unpack!"

Joe is a sentimental guy who loves the 1940s movie It's A Wonderful Life, and his motto is "home is where the heart is." So it's no wonder that he often reflects on the past highlights of his career.

One of these highlights was when the group appeared on the Arsenio Hall Show. A big fan of the movie Coming To America, Joe was really excited about meeting Arsenio. "He was hilarious," the 16-year-old recalls. "He was really funny and he pumped us up a lot for the performance. He gave

33

Not only does the group keep Joe busy, he still has one year of high school left. *Ernie Paniccioli*

us a really good introduction as well . . . and before we left, he said to us, 'Anytime you want to plug a new single or project, just come right back.' We just really had a good time with him. He's great to be around. He's a really funny guy."

Joe also reminisces about the occasional fan whom he actually gets to make friends with. "Every once in a while," he explains, "you meet a fan whom you get along well with and they take you around their city and show you the best spots. That's fun!"

In his spare time, Joe has to do his homework, and he says his favorite date activities are to just "chill out" and go skiing. He loves to watch reruns of *Cheers* and often needs to be pulled away from the "boob tube" to go to sound checks.

Joe is the smallest New Kid—but his heart is as big as they come. He's happy being the "little brother" on the block and hopes it continues forever. To him, life is one big block party—and all the New Kids' fans are invited!

Jordan receives lots of fan mail telling him he looks like a young Elvis or Paul McCartney. *Ernie Paniccioli*

# Jordan Knight
## *The "Knight" In Shining Armor!*

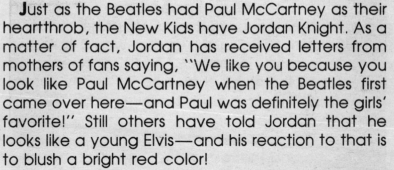

Just as the Beatles had Paul McCartney as their heartthrob, the New Kids have Jordan Knight. As a matter of fact, Jordan has received letters from mothers of fans saying, "We like you because you look like Paul McCartney when the Beatles first came over here—and Paul was definitely the girls' favorite!" Still others have told Jordan that he looks like a young Elvis—and his reaction to that is to blush a bright red color!

Born on May 17, 1971, Jordan, like Danny, is a hardworking Taurus. He's got a strong will and can do anything he puts his mind to, even if it requires a lot of self-discipline and sacrifice. Donnie calls him "the best singer in the group," which Jordan denies, but appreciates the compliment nevertheless!

Jordan describes himself this way: "I guess I'm the most 'normal' guy in the group. I'm basically an easygoing, laid-back guy."

37

In his spare time, Jordan can be found practicing his singing and shopping for clothes. He likes to buy shirts that mix the colors blue, red and black and he likes listening to classic soul singing groups from the '60s and '70s. The Stylistics are his favorite and have been since he was a little kid.

He says his faults are being a chronic nail biter and putting his foot in his mouth at times by being a little too truthful.

Jordan has "dreamer" qualities and admits he loves to be off in his own little world—something teachers didn't appreciate too much when he was still in school! He reminisces, "Long before I joined the group, I used to listen to the radio and say, 'I wish that could be me.' I used to dream of myself up onstage."

But when he had the opportunity to join the group he almost passed, because, as he puts it, "I was afraid that joining the group would take me away from all of my friends, and I really enjoyed hangin' with them. But then I came to my senses . . . I wanted to do it, and I became a full-fledged member after that."

Jordan not only gets along terrifically with his brother Jon and the rest of the New Kids, but he's got a terrific gift for making friends with people. He's always interested in learning about the lifestyles of people around the world, and touring has given him that golden opportunity.

Jordan loves performing, but he hopes to be a record producer one day. "I'm happy to be a singer now," says the tenor, "but when I get older, I want to produce some of my own groups. Like what happened with me and Maurice Starr taking a personal interest in my talents . . . I'd like to do that for someone else someday. But first I want to

While all the group members share a mutual respect for each other, Donnie says Jordan is a very hard worker. *Ernie Paniccioli*

become big as a singer." As a member of the Crickets—the studio name for Jordan, Donnie and Danny's production/songwriting/engineering team —Jordan coproduced the track "My Favorite Girl" on *Hangin' Tough.* So you can get an idea of how far his production talents have already come!

Jordan says he loves his work and doesn't mind the sacrifices he has had to make in his personal life to become a success. "Success feels kind of weird, but we're very happy that we're getting it because we've worked so hard for so long. We're not an overnight sensation—we've been doing this for four years and we've finally gotten our break. We feel good. All our hard work has paid off."

Jordan loves to perform and hopes to become a record producer. *Ernie Paniccioli*

Jordan loves reading fan mail, and a lot of it makes him chuckle. He gets the most fan mail of all the guys, so he feels doubly bad when he can't answer it all. He observes, "Around prom season, a lot of people write to us asking us to go to their proms. Also, when our birthdays come around, it's great. We get so many presents. It's nice to know so many people care about us."

Jordan says that he thinks of all those people that care about him when he gets a little homesick on the road. He confesses, "Sometimes we miss our parents and our homes and our friends from the neighborhood, and that's when I think about all the fans who care about us and who have written in—it's a real boost knowing how they feel and that some of them will be in the next town we're playing."

Of course, some of the fans have gotten a little out of hand and have thrown jellybeans up at the stage or have "made scenes" at airports and shopping malls, but Jordan understands that in their own strange way, they're trying to show they care. Still, security has become a big issue with the boys, and their management feels that it's better to be safe than sorry.

Jordan likes to philosophize about success, and like the other Kids, he's got a really down-to-earth approach to it: "I never set out to be a 'star.' We're just doing this because we love to be on-stage and to make people happy. Definitely the best part of being in this business is being onstage. We're here to entertain people, and that's what keeps us going."

He adds, on a serious note: "Sometimes I just wish I was a regular kid playing football with my friends after school . . . basically, just having a 'regular' life. Sometimes you think about those things because you miss them. But there are so many advantages to being in this business that there have to be a few disadvantages!"

One of the other disadvantages that actually gives Jordan a laugh is the tour bus the guys had when they were starting out on the road with Tiffany last year. "The first week on tour, our bus broke down five or six times. One time it got stuck in the mud and we had to get a tractor to pull it out. But things have gotten better."

Undoubtedly, they have . . . and they will get even better if the New Kids' success stays at its current level. As Jordan concludes with a smile, "All I want to do is prove that the New Kids aren't a joke—no matter what it takes!"

The New Kids visited Central Park on one of their trips to New York City. From left to right are Donnie, Jon, Joe, Jordan and Danny. *Robin Platzer, Images*

# From Around the Block to Around the World
## Life on the Road

It's true—before the New Kids became successful, they never got to see much of the country, let alone the world. As a matter of fact, Donnie had never been outside of Boston before joining the New Kids! To say that things have changed is an understatement, for in the last year, the New Kids have played virtually the whole free world, including Japan and Australia.

At first, they were wide-eyed innocents who felt out of place in sophisticated towns like Paris and Rome. But now, since they're on their third or fourth trips to those places, they're "travel professionals." If they ever left the music business, they would undoubtedly be top candidates for travel agent positions. They even know the best way to pack when going on a world tour. Joe can easily fit 15 shirts and a dozen pairs of jeans—not to mention a couple of weeks' worth of clean underwear and socks—into a standard-size suitcase. Fortunately, the better stage clothes are kept in a steamer trunk by the group's wardrobe person, who can often be found ironing outfits backstage about an hour before show time.

Being in a traveling band has not only been an educational and recreational experience for the group, but it has made them mature beyond their years. They've learned how to be part of a team—which not only includes one another, but a network of road managers and sound technicians. The Kids also have become ultra-organized—each of them gets a daily itinerary book of where they'll be traveling that day, the size of the venue, interview times and even who'll be backstage to "schmooze" on a certain night. The guys have countless responsibilities on the road, the most important ones being showing up for sound checks and print, TV and radio interviews. The work is carefully divided up, especially in terms of interviews, so that one Kid doesn't get any more media attention than another.

The boys are well adjusted to this hectic schedule, and every six weeks or so get to go home and live a normal life for anywhere from a few days to two weeks—but never long enough to unpack! The New Kids' managers like to keep their tour itinerary jam-packed, and if there's a demand for them in a certain part of the country at a certain time, a vacation day will quickly be canceled and a concert slated.

During the month of July, the Kids traveled to 13 states to perform in various places. Talk about a busy schedule.

Perhaps the road is hardest for Danny 'cause he's the only guy with a girlfriend back in Boston.

But nevertheless, Danny wouldn't have his life any other way! Although it may sound like a contradiction, touring is exhilarating and exhausting at the same time.

More than half the time on tour is spent traveling to the venue, and when the Kids have to travel under 500 miles, they "bus" it. There are actually two buses—one for the crew, and one for the Kids and their two bodyguards. Danny says, "Our tour buses are just like home. You have the living room, VCR, stereo, refrigerator, cooler, bathroom, and there are the beds. We love it." And of course the cellular phones, which the boys call home on twice a day!

There are exciting moments offstage as well. In every town the group visits, dozens to hundreds of fans get ahold of flight information and then greet the Kids at the airport. The boys never object to having their pictures snapped with fans at airports unless, of course, they're running late to the show or to an appointment. As a matter of fact, on a recent message on the Kids' 900-number hotline, Donnie apologized to fans who approached the guys at the wrong time. "We love you and we wish we could meet everyone, but time doesn't allow it. Maybe we'll meet in the future. Remember, we appreciate everything you've done for us and we're thinking of you all the time!"

Sometimes the group gets as many as five-hundred phone calls per day at their hotel—and other hotels in the area are often plagued with dozens of phone calls from fans trying to trace the Kids down. This has led the boys to having to use aliases—which have included the names of TV characters.

Donnie's the ringleader onstage and although

he doesn't have the most solos, he does the most emceeing. He'll start each show by screaming the town's name and driving the audience into a frenzy. For instance, last April in Orlando he shouted, "Orlando, are you ready to rock 'n' roll?" at the beginning of the show and was answered with a resounding "Yes!" Over 1,000 girls headed to the front of the stage and were asked politely to sit down.

A famous 1970 hit goes, "The road is long, with many a winding turn . . . " The New Kids have learned this many times over, and they can handle every "winding turn" with ease. In just a few short years, they've become consummate professionals. It's been a long trip from going around the block to going around the world, but the kids have enjoyed every minute of it—and have learned invaluable lessons along the way. So what if it's a little tough to sleep on a tour bus? It's a small price to pay for all the love and devotion they receive from fans who are anxious to see them live.

The New Kids participate in a few charity fundraisers. They are active in United Cerebral Palsy. From left to right are Joe, Jon, Danny, Donnie and Jordan. *Ernie Paniccioli*

Unlike some singing groups, the New Kids consider friendship the most important thing in their relationship. From left to right are Joe, Danny, Jon, Donnie and Jordan. *Ernie Paniccioli*

# Friends First . . . and Forever

Throughout this book, we've been caught up in all the excitement that just "comes with the territory" of being in a hugely popular pop group like New Kids on the Block. They're caught up in the excitement too, but through it all, they remember one thing: their friendship comes first.

This is a very unusual thing among singing groups. In most groups, members are easily replaced, and the audience usually accepts the new member without much complaining. But if the New Kids were ever to drop and/or add a new member, it would be a huge shock to fans, and things would probably never be the same again.

Donnie is the first to admit that friendship is what kept the guys together during the first three to four years, when they weren't exactly giant hit makers and there were many weeks between shows. "Friendship still plays a big role today. It's been said a million times before, but we're like brothers."

Donnie adds, with a smile, that the audience has grown up with them—and, happily, has grown consistently more mixed as time goes on. "Since we formed four years ago, our audience has developed with us. We all grew up in racially mixed neighborhoods, and when we started out doing local dates in Boston, our audience was 99-percent black. But since we got a chance to go on tour with Tiffany, our base has grown to include a lot of young, white teenaged girls."

The true test of friendship for a pop group is whether they hang out together even when they're off the road. Joe affirms the fact that the guys always hang out together when they're at home. "We'd be friends even if we weren't in a group, I feel. If this all ended tomorrow, we'd still want to see each other."

This *doesn't* mean that they always get along perfectly, but they only fight for brief periods. "We'll have a fight one night on the bus, and by the time the morning has rolled around, it'll be over . . . like it never happened. We can never not speak to each other for very long."

The Kids show a lot of affection for one another in their photos, videos and concerts, and not even a tiny bit of it is faked. Since they're all from big families, they've known what it's like to be really affectionate—and not think it looks "sissy-ish," like some guys their age believe.

Isn't it nice to know that there's a group where the feelings between the members are genuine. Says Joe, "I read about guys in rock groups who don't even talk to each other . . . where each member has his own bus, and I can't believe it. The really sad part is that most of those guys got along before they got famous—and then egos got in the way and it all fell apart. That will never happen to us—we have too much of a sense of reality about us. There are no star trips at all—and if anyone ever got one, they'd be put in line immediately by both the other guys and our manager, Dick Scott."

It's obvious to the New Kids that "hangin' tough" means "hangin' *together*," and they have a message of peace, love and understanding.

The New Kids, (l-r) Jon, Joe, Donnie, Jordan and Danny, recently performed at the Palladium in New York City at Z-100's sixth anniversary party. *Robin Platzer, Images*

# "Tough" Times Ahead
## *Looking to the Future*

The New Kids want nothing more from the future than for their present success to continue. Their favorite aspect of success is the live shows, and they will do anything to keep the shows fresh and exciting—or, as they would put it, "funky fresh!"

The guys are always changing around their nightly song lists. Even though they definitely perform their hits at every concert, the Kids like to throw in surprise songs that might be "blasts from the past" or brand-new material they've never performed in public before. Jordan remarks, "Through all his years of writing songs, our producer Maurice Starr has accumulated a whole library of songs to pick and choose from. When we go in to record an album, we have like 100 songs to pick from, and then we record the 10 most suited to our sound."

And speaking of recording, the guys will be doing another album in spring '90—providing their tour doesn't get extended, thus pushing up the recording date. Donnie says he looks forward to doing the next album and thinks it's interesting how the group's sound matures as time goes on—especially Joe's sound, which took a unique twist after his voice changed in '87!

Jordan says, "We hope to be playing instruments on the next album. We're practicing during sound check everyday and when we're at home. And of course we'll be continuing with our behind-the-scenes interests . . . like me with producing and Danny with engineering. Donnie's working on writing songs. It'll be interesting to hear Maurice's critique of them!"

Touring will always be the Kids' focus, however, and most of '90 will be taken up with headlining gigs at arenas (musical friends Dino and Sweet Sensation will be the openers). Donnie says, "The venue we're most looking forward to is the Boston Garden. We've played there before, but it wasn't the same thing because we were opening for Jeffrey Osbourne and the Pointer Sisters, but weren't the headliners. All our friends and family will be there."

Also on the horizon for the Kids are countless TV show appearances, and they can't wait to go back on *the Arsenio Hall Show.* The guys have already taped two shows for the Disney Channel's *New Mickey Mouse Club* and hope to do their own Disney special next summer, although right now nothing's been confirmed.

And, of course, there'll be videos made for all the New Kids' forthcoming hit singles. At press time, they're enjoying the success of the video for the Christmas hit "This One's for the Children," which is featured heavily on Nickelodeon and other youth-oriented cable networks.

Donnie reflects on the future: "We thank God for what we have every day—and we also pray for it to continue. More than anything else, I'd like to be taken more seriously. There's still the few people who think of us as a teenybop act or something."

Jordan adds with a serious look on his face, "I want to continue the success that we're having and I want to stay New Kids on the Block for a long time. I don't want the group to break up or to go solo. I think it would be a mistake for the guys to do solo projects."

It looks like the New Kids have only good things to look forward to in the future—including New Kids on the Block Day, which was proclaimed by Governor Michael Dukakis to be April 24. All the New Kids and their hometown fans will be gathered around a famous Boston landmark—probably the Boston Commons—to celebrate!

The New Kids not only have the key to the city of Boston, but the key to the whole pop world at this point . . . and they couldn't be happier. They've traveled from around the block to around the world with their sweet harmonies, and their reaction to the experience is simply, "It's tough!"

When the New Kids say "tough," it's a *good* thing—it means "cooler than cool." We hope they have a lot of "tough" times ahead! Fans will be waiting for their next album and tour, for these Beantown boys only get better with age! Keep "hangin' tough," dudes!

# Vital Stats You Can't Live Without!

The New Kids take a few moments to relax backstage at the Westbury Music Fair.   *Robin Platzer, Images*

## *Joseph Mulrey McIntyre*

**Birthdate:**  December 31, 1972
**Hair Color:**  Brown
**Eye Color:**  Blue
**Height:**  5'6"
**Weight:**   125 pounds
**Favorite Saying:**  Word up!
**Favorite Food:**  Anything Italian

**Favorite Drink:** Soda water with lime
**Favorite Date Activities:** Just chillin' out (relaxing) and skiing
**Future Plans:** To be happy and live a good life

## Jonathan Rasleigh Knight

**Birthdate:** November 29, 1968
**Hair Color:** Brown
**Eye Color:** Hazel
**Height:** 5'11"
**Weight:** 160 pounds
**Favorite Saying:** Where's Peter? (referring to road manager Peter Work)
**Favorite Food:** McDonald's
**Favorite Drink:** Strawberry Shake
**Favorite Date Activities:** Anything goes!
**Future Plans:** To continue with the New Kids until they can no longer sing

## Jordan Nathaniel Marcel Knight

**Birthdate:** May 17, 1971
**Hair Color:** Brown
**Eye Color:** Brown
**Height:** 5'10"
**Weight:** 155 Pounds
**Favorite Saying:** We'll be alright
**Favorite Food:** Snack food and Mexican
**Favorite Drink:** Chocolate milkshake
**Favorite Date Activity:** Going to the beach

57

**Future Plans:** To stay happy and prove that the New Kids are no joke!

## Donnie Wahlberg

**Birthdate:** August 17, 1969
**Hair Color:** Blond
**Eye Color:** Hazel
**Height:** 5'11"
**Weight:** 155 Pounds
**Favorite Saying:** Peace out!
**Favorite Food:** Italian
**Favorite Drink:** Water
**Favorite Date Activity:** A quiet dinner, with a walk around Boston afterwards
**Future Plans:** To be the best I can be, and to make the Northside Posse (a rap group I produce) get really big!

## Daniel Wood

**Birthdate:** May 14, 1970
**Hair Color:** Black
**Eye Color:** Brown
**Height:** 5'7½"
**Weight:** 152 Pounds
**Favorite Sayings:** Hang tough; I'm outta here!
**Favorite Foods:** Mexican, Chinese and Italian
**Favorite Drink:** Strawberry shake
**Favorite Date Activity:** Taking a walk
**Future Plans:** To take things one day at a time and learn as much as possible

# New Kids Quiz

**W**ant to test your New Kids' I.Q.? Then answer the following questions, and check your answers against the answer key on page 61.

1. The New Kids' manager's name is: a) Kevin Kennedy b) Win Wilford c) Dick Scott d) Mark Wahlberg
2. The New Kids have released how many albums?: a) One b) Two c) Three d) Four
3. What famous pop princess has the group toured with many times?: a) Debbie Gibson b) Paula Abdul c) Tiffany d) Martika
4. Which of the following do all the New Kids have in common: a) They all come from large families b) They're all the same age c) They all think being on the road is a drag d) They all wish they could move to New York
5. Which of the following songs is *not* a New Kids hit?: a) "My Prerogative" b) "Cover Girl" c) "Please Don't Go Girl" d) "You Got It (The Right Stuff)"
6. What are Donnie's favorite colors?: a) Black and gold b) Black and white

59

c) Brown and gold d) Purple and yellow

7. Name the two brothers in the group:
   a) Jon and Jordan b) Jon and Joe c)
   Danny and Joe d) Danny and Donnie

8. Name the first guy selected by producer Maurice Starr to join the group:
   a) Donnie b) Danny c) Jordan d) Jon

9. Who runs the New Kids' "official" fan
   club in Quincy, MA?: a) Dick Scott
   Entertainment b) Info-tainment, Inc.
   c) Their mothers d) Columbia Records

10. What day did Governor Michael Du-
    kakis declare as New Kids on the
    Block Day?: a) April 24 b) May 1 c)
    June 16 d) July 5

11. Which Kid has sisters who are ac-
    tresses? a) Joe b) Donnie c) Danny
    d) Jordan

12. Which Kid auditioned for the group
    by doing a Michael Jackson imperso-
    nation?: a) Jon b) Jordan c) Donnie
    d) Joe

13. What is the name of the New Kids'
    Christmas LP?: a) *Jingle Bells* b) *Merry,
    Merry Christmas* c) *The New Kids'
    Christmas Album* d) *Have Yourself A
    Merry Little Christmas*

14. When Danny, Donnie and Jordan
    work together in the studio produc-
    ing, writing and playing instruments,
    they call themselves: a) The Crickets
    b) The Jamaican Dog Posse c) The
    Beetles d) The Northside Posse

15. What is the name of the group Donnie
    is producing?: a) The Northside Posse

b) Def Duo c) Centipede d) The Mice Posse

16. Donnie and Jordan are the same height. They're: a) 5'8" b) 5'11" c) 6' d) 6'11"

17. Which two kids are huge fans of the Fox TV show *America's Most Wanted?*: a) Danny and Jordan b) Donnie and Jordan c) Danny and Joe d) Jon and Jordan

18. The group's original name was: a) Nynuk b) The Crazy Crew c) M.C. Donnie W. and the Funky Fresh Crew d) The Knight Bros. Revue

19. The group's only complaint about touring is that: a) They don't get enough sleep b) They don't meet enough fans c) They have no time to work out d) They have to do too many interviews

**Answer Key**

1. c, 2. c, 3. c, 4. a, 5. a, 6. a, 7. a, 8. a, 9. c, 10. a, 11. a, 12. c, 13. b, 14. a, 15. a, 16. b, 17. a, 18. a, and 19. a, .

*Scoring*

15 or more right: You're a *real* New Kids fan!
10-14 right: Not bad, but maybe you'd better go back and reread this book.
Below 10 right: Are you sure you're a fan? If so, you'd better join up with The New Kids Fan Club and brush up on your facts!

# "Blockbusters"
## A New Kids Discography

*New Kids on the Block* (Columbia Records)—Released December 1986 Features: "Stop It Girl"; "Didn't I (Blow Your Mind)?"; "Popsicle"; "Angel"; "Be My Girl"; "New Kids on the Block"; "Are You Down?"; "I Wanna Be Loved by You"; "Don't Give Up on Me"; and "Treat Me Right."

Singles released off this album were (in consecutive order):

"Be My Girl"; "Stop It Girl"; and "Didn't I (Blow Your Mind)?"

*Hangin' Tough* (Columbia Records)—Released March 1988 Features: "You Got It (The Right Stuff)"; "Please Don't Go Girl"; "I'll Be Loving You (Forever)"; "Cover Girl"; "I Neéd You"; "Hangin' Tough"; "I Remember When"; "What'cha Gonna Do (About It)"; "My Favorite Girl"; and "Hold On."

Singles released off this album were (in consecutive order):

"Please Don't Go Girl"; "You Got It (The Right Stuff)"; "I'll Be Loving You (Forever)"; "Hangin' Tough" (b/w "Didn't I (Blow Your Mind)?" from the first album); and "Cover Girl."

*Merry, Merry Christmas* (Columbia Records)—Released September 1989 Features: "This One's for the Children"; "Last Night I Saw Santa Claus"; "I'll Be Missin' You Come Christmas (A Letter to Santa)"; "I Still Believe in Santa Claus"; "Merry, Merry Christmas"; "The Christmas Song (Chestnuts Roasting on an Open Fire)"; "Funky, Funky Xmas"; "White Christmas"; "Little Drummer Boy"; and "This One's for the Children (Reprise)."
Singles released as of 9/89: "This One's for the Children."
(More to follow throughout the Christmas season)

## Videography

Short-form videos exist for all the singles. The Kids have released one long-form video (available from CMV Enterprises/CBS Music Video Enterprises), which is a compilation of the hit videos for "Please Don't Go Girl," "You Got It (The Right Stuff)," "I'll Be Loving You (Forever)"; and "Hangin' Tough." It was released in July '89.

The New Kids put a lot of time and effort into their work as they
practice their songs and dance routines for a future concert. From
left to right are Joe, Jon, Donnie, Danny and Jordan.
*Ernie Paniccioli*